RESTLESS SPIRIT

THE HOLY SPIRIT FROM A PROCESS PERSPECTIVE

BRUCE G. EPPERLY

Topical Line Drives #48

Energion Publications
Gonzalez, Florida
2022

ISBN: 978-1-63199-824-9
eISBN: 978-1-63199-825-6

Energion Publications
PO Box 841
Gonzalez, FL 32560

https://energion.com
pubs@energion.com

TABLE OF CONTENTS

1	The Many Faces of the Spirit	2
2	Creative Spirit	8
3	Unfettered Spirit	12
4	Global Spirit	18
5	Guiding Spirit	24
6	Prophetic Spirit	29
7	Healing Spirit	33
8	The Further Adventures of the Spirit	36

THE MANY FACES OF THE SPIRIT

> Jesus said to them again, "Peace be with you. As the
> Father has sent me, so I send you." When he had said this, he
> breathed on them and said to them, "Receive the Holy Spirit.
> (John 20:21-22)

We don't hear much about the Holy Spirit in progressive
churches. Nor is the Holy Spirit the focus of most texts by process theologians. Process theologians, like most liberal Christians,
seldom place the Holy Spirit at the center of their theological
reflection. Process theology's most innovative theological work has
involved articulating transformative visions of God as relational
and non-coercive, the fellow sufferer who understands, and Christ
as the principle of creative transformation, naturalistically present
in all creation. Process theology has challenged traditional visions
of God as omnipotent, unchanging, and punitive. Process theologians have led the way in formulating naturalistic and universalist
understandings of creation, Christology, sacrament, and healing.
They have charted the dimensions of a God-filled universe through
their affirmation that Christ's impact and mission range far beyond
institutional Christianity, inspiring every quest for personal wholeness and social justice under whatever guise it appears. But, for
the most part, witness to the Holy Spirit has been silent in process
circles.[1]

For many progressive Christians and process theologians, the
Holy Spirit has been an afterthought, found typically at the margins
of our theological reflection or neglected completely as irrelevant
in relation to more pressing theological, social, economic, and
environmental issues. While there have been exceptions among
process theologians, reflections on the Trinity have also tended
to be an add-on or have been articulated in ways that awkwardly

---

1 Process theologians addressing the Trinity include: Joseph Bracken and
   Marjorie Suchocki, *Trinity in Process: A Relational Theology of God* (New
   York: Continuum, 1997) and Norman Pittenger, *The Divine Triunity* (New
   York: United Church Press, 1977),

describe the Trinity in terms of process categories, such as connecting the three persons of the Trinity with the primordial (eternal and unchanging), consequent (relational and constantly changing), and superjective (incarnational and contextual) natures of God.

I must confess, as a theologian and pastor, the Holy Spirit and Trinity have been at the periphery of my writing and preaching. In the conservative Baptist congregation of my childhood, we focused on the sovereignty of God, obeying God's law in our individual lives, and the necessity of a personal relationship with Jesus for our salvation and the salvation of our loved ones. To the Baptists of my childhood, God had no concern for the non-human world except as a prop for human industry or a means of experiencing God's grandeur. I can't recall celebrating Pentecost or hearing a sermon on the Holy Spirit until graduate school. If we spoke of the Holy Spirit at all, we identified the Spirit with Pentecostal "holy rollers" and the theatrical ministries of Oral Roberts and Kathryn Kuhlman. The Spirit lived up to her alter ego, "Ghost," and was as theologically diaphanous and intermittent as a specter.

I began seriously to consider the Holy Spirit when I started studying the healing ministry of Jesus in the context of how progressive Christians might understand these miraculous moments in Jesus' ministry. To be a savvy scholar, conversant with the varieties of Christian and non-Christian healing, I needed to know about Oral Roberts, Kathryn Kuhlman, and Benny Hinn and study their claims to embody Jesus' healing ministry in our time. Still, I never felt comfortable with the Spirit they peddled: supernaturally intervening in certain peoples' lives while neglecting others, arbitrary and sporadic in its manifestations, speaking in odd and incomprehensible tongues, being uniquely available to those who contributed most generously to the particular televangelist's healing ministry, and punishing people with illness for their lack of faith or inability to live within the stated ethical norms of conservative Christianity.

In considering the Spirit's role in Christian experience, many progressive and mainstream Christians are uncomfortable with the company she keeps — Pentecostals, Second Coming preachers, Christian nationalists, wily witnesses, and spiritual snake oil salespersons. We are concerned with the fact that many popular pastors identify the Holy Spirit solely with their brand of Pentecostalism and its tendency toward wild worship, speaking in tongues, and spiritual elitism. We are also troubled by the attraction to the prosperity gospel and conservative, nation-first politics among an array of Pentecostal luminaries. A few of us have come to affirm a different type of Pentecostalism, not flamboyant, partisan, or commercialized, but focused on Spirit as guide, companion, inspiration, and challenge to every status quo, including our unacknowledged idolatry, racism, and complacency with environmental destruction and injustice.

As a process theologian, I have often asserted that margins can become the frontiers. I believe at this point in our history, this may be true for the Holy Spirit. Her marginal status, and absence in our usual theological reflection, may challenge us to go beyond the familiar and controllable into the adventurous and mystical. Movements of the Spirit, understood as invitational, naturalistic, and transformative, may be exactly what process and progressive Christianity needs as we face an unprecedented time of pandemic, cultural divisiveness, and global climate change. The Spirit is mysterious and unfettered. While the free-ranging movements of God's Spirit do not lend themselves to a systematic theology, embracing this lively Spirit may be what we need to animate our churches and spirituality to face the congregational, national, and planetary challenges ahead. We may need her "out of the box" and "out of the church" energy to propel us into new ways of congregational and ethical imagination and action.

An Adventurous Trinity. Any reflection on the Holy Spirit compels us to consider the Holy Trinity. The Trinity makes some bold and audacious claims about God's inner life and outward activities. God is One and yet Three. The Creator/Creative Energy and Wisdom in All Things is also flesh and blood in our world. Incarnate in Galilee, Christ is also energetically and innovatively present in and through all things. The Spirit is a challenge to all those who want clear theological definitions. Augustine once noted that "if you think you know it, it isn't God" but a human-shaped God we can

4

fully fathom and thus seek to control. Augustine's counsel surely applies to the freewheeling, completely unbounded Spirit of God.

Progressive Christians are in many ways unitarian in spirit, believing a literal threeness is irrelevant to our understanding of God. Yet the scriptures speak of Spirit as central to the formation and growth of the Jesus movement and point to multiplicity within God's nature. We have moments of spiritual energy that transform us. Although potentially present everywhere and in all persons, such spirit-filled moments are not uniform in our own spiritual journeys or in the autobiographies of mystics and social activists. Might we expect the same variety in divine manifestations?

As I reflect on the Trinity, I believe that divine unity and plurality are important. Though consistently one in moral character and intent, seeking wholeness and Shalom in every situation, God is also many-faceted in impact and presence. As reflections of divine wisdom, we are also one and many-faceted, relating to life in many ways and experiencing the grace of God in diverse and contrasting manners. We are legion, abounding in possibility, initiating novelty, and expressing ourselves creatively, and so is God.

The "most moved" mover of process theology is also the ultimate pluralist and relativist. The Personal God, who inspired the quest for a personal relationship with Jesus in the church of my childhood, is also the shape-shifting God, appearing concretely as the source of creative transformation in ways suited to our condition, as the Quakers assert.[2]

Spirit Abounding. The Pentecost need not be Pentecostal, nor should we identify the spirit with the status quo, whether that of our own theologies or congregations or any other. As you will see in my meditations on John 3 and Acts 2, Spirit is free, iconoclastic, justice-seeking, unifying, universal, and beyond binary understandings of truth, doctrine, and salvation. In fact, the least spirited behaviors and doctrines are often perpetuated by those claiming to hold the keys of orthodoxy and biblical truth. The moment you locate the Spirit in one practice, community, or experience, she shows us in an entirely different location and among people whose practices contrast with your own. While the Spirit of truth ranges

2 For an insightful discussion of the Trinity, see Chris Eyre, *A Holy Mystery: Taking Apart the Trinity* (Gonzalez, FL: Energion Publications, 2019)

through all creation and inspires our spiritual adventures, the Spirit is never orthodox or homogenous. Accordingly, the free-spirited nature of the Holy Spirit defies formulating a systematic pneumatology. We can see traces of Spirit — Spirit sightings — in the same way as we see wind rustling through the leaves or propelling waves to the shoreline. Everywhere and acting in various ways, intimately tailored to our openness and life situation, the Spirit addresses each of us personally. Often, however, we fail to see these traces of Spirit, subtly shaping our lives and providentially moving in synchronous encounters.

The Spirit is spiritual and experiential, not dogmatic. As in the case of the experiences of Jesus' first followers, described in Acts of the Apostles, Spirit pushes doctrine to the limit, forcing us to make it up as we go along.[3] Encountering God is more important than words about God. The flames and winds of Spirit burst beyond tradition, dogma, clergy, church, and sacrament. Spirit goes and flows, breathing and moving in everything, from the non-human world to the meditations of our hearts.

In the pages ahead, I will seek to describe Spirit-sightings in my own life, in scripture, and among those who intuited Spirit in their spiritual pilgrimages. It was appropriate that this text emerged from my weekly Theological and Spiritual Reflection seminar sponsored by South Congregational Church, United Church of Christ, on Cape Cod, Massachusetts, but also attended via Zoom by persons in Oregon, Colorado, Maryland, and New York. Although we were physically distant due to our commitment to safe and whole-person mission in a time of pandemic, we experienced an intimacy characteristic of the Spirit's movements in our lives. These reflections also emerged during a time of protest following the death of George Floyd on May 25, 2020, an event that graphically revealed the ongoing structural injustice and violence, born of America's "original sin" of racism, often perpetuated by white Christians.[4] Spirit challenges every structure that dehumanizes and

3 For a process and mystical interpretation of Acts of the Apostles, see Bruce Epperly, *Transforming Acts: The Acts of the Apostles as a Twenty-first Century Gospel* (Gonzales, FL: Energion Publications, 2013).

4 See Robert P. Jones, *White Too Long: The Legacy of White Supremacy in American Christianity* (New York: Simon and Schuster, 2020).

destroys the foundations of human wholeness and fulfillment. The mysticism of the Spirit drives us from the sanctuary to the streets in solidarity with those whose spirits have been crushed by institutional injustice, even when it is perpetrated by our nation and people who claim to be Christians.

My approach in reflecting on the Spirit will be meditative, emerging from the interplay of scripture and spiritual experience in the context of the troubled, uncertain, yet Spirit-filled, world of protest and pandemic. So, I begin this spiritual adventure by invoking the Spirit's guidance and saying "thank you" to a congregation that supported my vocation as a theologian seeking the Spirit's enlivening illumination in the words and meditations of this text.

> Breathe on me, Breath of God,
> Fill me with life anew,
> That I may love what Thou dost love,
> And do what Thou wouldst do.
> Breathe on me, Breath of God,
> Until my heart is pure,
> Until with Thee I will one will,
> To do and to endure.
> Breathe on me, Breath of God,
> Till I am wholly Thine,
> Until this earthly part of me
> Glows with Thy fire divine.[5]

---

5 Edwin Hatch, *Breathe on Me, Breath of God (1878)*

CHAPTER TWO

CREATIVE SPIRIT

In the beginning when God created the heavens and the earth, the earth was a formless void and darkness covered the face of the deep, while the Spirit of God swept over the face of the waters. Then God said, "Let there be light"; and there was light… Then God said, "Let us make humankind in our image, according to our likeness; and let them have dominion over the fish of the sea, and over the birds of the air, and over the cattle, and over all the wild animals of the earth, and over every creeping thing that creeps upon the earth."

So God created humankind in the divine image, in the image of God he created them; male and female God created them. (Genesis 1:1-3, 26-27, AP)

My reflections on the Holy Spirit emerged from the interplay of my own spiritual and theological pilgrimage and the insights of a Zoom Class focusing on the Holy Spirit. As a relational and interactive teacher, I always try to connect classes with the experiences of participants and let their questions be guideposts for our journey together.

Accordingly, at our first gathering, I asked the gathered participants, "what comes to mind when you think of the Holy Spirit?" Their responses included: wisdom, guidance, divine energy, spirit within, unexpected inspiration, helper, animating force of the universe, and the still small voice. When I asked if they had any negative reactions to the Holy Spirit, one responded that many "Spirit-filled people use the phrase, 'God told me' to justify irrational and violent behavior." Another added, "some people use their experiences of the Holy Spirit to assume they are spiritually superior to others. They believe that they have the truth while others are lost." She continued, "encounters with Spirit should encourage humility rather than pride and relationship rather than judgment."

Throughout history and in our time, encounters with the Holy Spirit are ambiguous like every other human endeavor. Revelation, even mystical revelation, requires a receiver who brings to their experience of the Spirit and the subsequent sharing of their experience of the Spirit, all their gifts and limitations, ethnic, historical, and spirituality. Our perspectives give concreteness to encounters with the Spirit. They may also limit the scope and impact of these encounters. Accordingly, our encounters with God's Spirit can give life and inspire love, but they can also be misused to foment violence and coercion and inspire spiritual elitism and superiority. Depending on our attitude toward Spirit-sightings, the flames of the Spirit can warm and inspire, and they can also enflame and destroy.

In the Beginning was the Spirit. The poetic cosmology of Genesis describes the Spirit of God moving over the primordial and unformed chaos, giving birth to the foundations of cosmic and human order and creativity. In the spirit of the Genesis creation story with which this chapter began, Divine Wisdom or Spirit (Chokmah, Sophia) described in Proverbs 8, is active from the very beginning of cosmic and planetary creation:

> beside God, like a master worker;
> and I was daily God's delight,
> rejoicing before the Creator always,
> rejoicing in God's inhabited world
> and delighting in the human race. (Proverbs 8:30-31,
> author's paraphrase)

Spirit is both infinite and intimate. Spirit is present at every level of the creative process, from the microscopic to the galactic. Spirit animates our cells as well as souls. Unbounded in creativity and inspiration, Spirit goes beyond the church and humankind alike to encompass all creation. Pastor-song writer Jim Manley captures the evolutionary energy of God's Spirit:

> Spirit, Spirit of gentleness, blow through the wilderness, calling and free. Spirit, Spirit of restlessness, stir me from placidness, Wind, Wind on the sea.
> You moved on the waters, you called to the deep, then you coaxed up the mountains from valleys of sleep, and over

the eons you called to each thing: Awake from your slumbers and rise on your wings.[6]

When we awaken from our spiritual slumbers, we experience creation declaring the glory of God. With awakened spirits, our gentle contemplation finds fulfillment in restless justice-seeking.

Spirit as Centered Pluralism. While much in scripture stretches the imagination and takes us into the mystic, the words describing God's creation of humankind in the first Genesis creation story take us into the realm of the mysterious and provocative.

> Let us make humankind in our image, according to our likeness… So God created humankind in the divine image, in the image of God he created them; male and female God created them.

Although resolving this mystery is above our theological paygrades and joins both the *kataphatic*, our ability to describe God in words, images, and doctrines, and the *apophatic*, the indescribability of God, I believe this passage points to plurality and multiplicity within divinity. In God's wondrous creativity, God is more than we can imagine. Within the divine there is a movement toward pluralistic, multidimensional creativity, which out of its fullness delights in the emergence and evolution of diverse galaxies, planets, flora, fauna, cultures, and human experiences. God is One and Centered. God is also Many and Diverse. God's creative wisdom, complex, dynamic, and evolving in relationship to creation parents forth a complex, dynamic, and evolving universe. To use the language of process theology, God is the constant engine of the creative transformation of the many into one and the one into the many.

God's integrity and oneness are manifold and each of the Persons of the Trinity joins unity and diversity in relationship to the others and the world. In the case of the Holy Spirit, the constant creativity and inspiration of God's Spirit touch each and every creature and moment lovingly and intimately beginning in the heart and then reaching out through our hands and caring for others. The gifts of the Spirit are Infinite and are manifest intimately in a

---

6 Jim Manley, "Spirit of Gentleness." Used by permission.

constant dialogue with each moment's emerging creative process. The Infinite is the Intimate, and the Eternal is the Everchanging as the Spirit's faithfulness and mercy are new every morning.

While it is appropriate to identify the Holy Spirit with Hokmah and Sophia, the feminine dimension of reality, the Trinitarian nature of God takes us beyond binary understandings of reality as female and male, gay and straight, cisgendered and transgendered, dark and light, human and non-human. The Yin and Yang of God spiral into "infinity and beyond," to quote Buzz Lightyear from "Toy Story." Centered in all things, God as Spirit flows pluralistically into everything and back again to unity only to flow multiply back giving energy and inspiration whether in the birth of a galaxy, a creative idea, or the experience of healing and salvation. Creative Spirit gives birth to galaxies and planets, cultures and religions, magi and midwives, and flora and fauna. Creative Spirit parents the breaching whale and the child transfixed in delight as she observes the sporting whale. Creative Spirit is never finished with the serious work of delighting and bringing forth delight in evolving of humankind and the non-human world, and the energetic movements of the moral and spiritual arc she inspires.

CHAPTER THREE

UNFETTERED SPIRIT

The law of the Spirit of life in Christ Jesus has set you free from the law of sin and death…you have received a spirit of freedom. (Romans 8:1-2, 15)

The one thing about the Holy Spirit that you can count on is that the Spirit is surprising, unpredictable, and untrammeled by human willfulness, church doctrine, or ritual. She is, as Jim Manley, intones, "calling and free." To the consternation and amazement of the Jewish spiritual leader Nicodemus, Jesus asserts:

The Spirit (wind) blows where it chooses, and you hear the sound of it, but you do not know where it comes or where it goes. So it is with everyone who is born of the Spirit. (John 3:8)

The Spirit sets us free. The Spirit frees us from the chains of dead doctrines and demonic structures. As the breath of life, Spirit may be gentle and unassuming, quietly calm during your morning meditation. Spirit may also be fierce, whipping through your spiritual and communal life with the force of a hurricane, turning everything upside down and demolishing familiar religious structures, protesting injustice, and crying "I can't breathe" to those who constrict the breathing of her children. Like Aslan from C.S. Lewis' *Chronicles of Narnia*, the Spirit of God is not safe, although Spirit is good, as it revives our spirits and sends us forth on pilgrimages toward new horizons of God's Holy Adventure.

When I led a *Lectio Divina* exercise in course of our theological reflection class at South Congregational Church, one of the participants responded to the John 3:8 passages with the words, "I don't get it!" I responded, "This is the point. Even though you don't get it, you've got it!" I reminded the class of Augustine's assertion that "if you think you know it, it isn't God." This surely applies to Jesus' description of the Spirit. God's Spirit is uncontrollable, unfathomable, and unfettered. You can't put the Spirit in a box or freeze-frame it in doctrines or institutional structures. If you try to confine it here, it shows up there. If you define it in one way, it shows up in another way. Spirit is always more than we can imagine or describe.

The unfettered Spirit inspires our own spiritual restlessness and creativity. The unbounded Spirit challenges every limitation we place on God's presence. Surely Nicodemus, a spiritual leader of an "organized religion," was initially troubled by Jesus' revolutionary words. If Spirit is free, like the wind, no religious institution can claim privilege. As important as the Jerusalem Temple is in the faith of the Jewish people, it is not the sole repository of faith. As significant as the Temple's impact is on the religious and cultural identity of the Jewish people, God can show up in new and creative ways, outside the Temple precincts and outside the boundaries of Judaism or today in our various flavors of Christianity. As important as your doctrines and denominations are in your spiritual formation, none can encompass or fulfill the Spirit's work. Spirit is always free, iconoclastic, and prophetic in its challenge to our current understandings of divine presence and inspiration.

On Pentecost, Jesus' first followers discovered that through the movements of God's Spirit, all the binary boundaries of in and out, saved and unsaved, and wise and unlettered are overcome. While I cannot claim to know the movements of the Spirit, or where she will show up next, I have felt God's Spirit propelling me to new horizons.

Sometimes the Spirit moves in times of anxiety and uncertainty. As a preteen, having recently relocated from the bucolic Salinas Valley to bustling San Jose, California, I initially attended a conservative Christian church in the neighborhood. Moving to San Jose after a family crisis turned my world upside down. Nothing was familiar and my family, which enjoyed professional status in small-town America, were nobodies in our new neighborhood. My parents sought refuge in the old-time religion, but I felt suffocated. I literally couldn't breathe during the religious services. I needed spiritual breathing space. Looking back over more than fifty-five years, I believe God's Spirit was present in alerting me to my spiritual — and physical — suffocation. I was being given a Spirit-sighting, although I had no words for it at the time. I was being awakened to my need for spiritual expansiveness and within a few years, I began both to intellectually and spiritually challenge the faith of my childhood through studies of American Transcendentalism, Asian religions, psychedelic adventures, Transcendental Meditation, and contemplative Christian spirituality, all of which provided the launching ground for the faith I affirm today. What was considered heresy in the conservative Christianity of my childhood became the bread of life to a teenage seeker and budding theologian.

Moved by the Spirit's "sighs too deep for words," I left the church only to rediscover it the week after learning Transcendental Meditation in 1970. Yet, repeating my TM mantra took me beyond Maharishi to rediscover Jesus and the riches of the Christian contemplative tradition in a lively questioning, theologically open, and socially active Baptist congregation.

Yet now even in my late sixties, the unfettered Spirit is pushing me to new horizons for which my spiritual GPS is still in search of direction. Alfred North Whitehead notes that the pure conservative is going against the nature of the universe. God's Spirit moves us forward and outward. While Spirit may call us to times of retreat, our withdrawals from the world are temporary and strategic and never complete. Our spiritual retreats are intended to remind us that the Spirit that centers us is the ever-expanding moving force in all creation, human and non-human, and that God's Spirit centers everyone, without exception, whether or not we are aware of the Spirit within us.

In these times of pandemic and protest, I personally have felt the restless and often uncomfortable movements of God's Spirit. Contemplative and scholarly by nature, my inclination is to encounter the world through images, thoughts, and words. I prefer the study to the picket line. I find meaning more in contemplation than in confrontation, and yet the Spirit is telling me that the truths I need to be of service to present and future generations will be found both in the walking in picket lines and the writing in solitude. During this time in which the future of our nation and planet is at stake, a spiritual restlessness is inviting me toward a new form of contemplative activism, motivated by the Spirit's call to prophetic healing.

Not known as a political activist, and preferring seminars to demonstrations and written pieces to protests, I am feeling the stirrings of Spirit to greater political activism in my emerging prophetic vocation as a gentle activist, claiming more fully my emerging calling, as God's companion in healing the world. While I do not know the path on which the Spirit is leading me, I do know that the Spirit is inspiring me to greater reflection issuing in action related to systemic racism and injustice, white privilege, income inequality, and poverty, First Nations genocide then and now, and global climate change. I have never "spoken in tongues" but I have become empathetic and attentive to God's voice speaking in the tongues and cadence of the vulnerable, marginalized, oppressed, and abused.

Ships of the Spirit are not intended to rest quietly in safe harbors but to launch out into restless seas, uncertain of the direction but shifting their sails to capture the unfettered winds of the Spirit. The Coronavirus pandemic has transformed congregational life. Protest has upended our national complacency. As treasured as our sanctuaries are to us, we have experienced God's untrammeled Spirit on Zoom, Instagram, and Facebook. We have discovered that there is nothing virtual about online worship. God's Spirit has touched our hearts and minds in Zoom worship and classes and has brought people together in new and transformational ways. The old ways of congregational worship have served us well and are inspiring, but Spirit moves us toward new encounters with God's transformative love and inspiration.

The response to the brutal murder of George Floyd appears also to be a movement of the Spirit. Embodied in the footsteps of protesters who are making it up as they go along, inspired by the call "Black Lives Matter" and blown forward by winds of the Spirit along city streets in Minneapolis, Los Angeles, Kenosha, Portland, Louisville, and Washington DC., Americans of all races are protesting and not just African Americans. Surely the Spirit moves through our fallible, and justifiably angry, struggles for freedom and equality for all! Though politicians and ministers bunker with their Bibles, blaming victims and inciting violence with thinly-veiled racist dog whistle language, the world is watching. Spirit is telling us about the "cross and the lynching tree." Spirit is joining concern for inequalities in health care and economic injustice during pandemic, disproportionately impacting African Americans, First Americans, and economically disadvantaged whites, with the realities of structural racism in police departments, educational institutions, and economic inequalities increasing even as we chant "we're all in this together."[7]

Spirit shouts through George Floyd's daughter Gianna when she says, "Dad changed the world." Spirit speaks through chants of "I can't breathe." Spirit laments through the voices of Parkland youth pleading for the opportunity to go to school without fearing gun violence. Spirit gusts in Greta Thunberg sailing across the Atlantic in a solar-powered yacht to challenge the apathy of adults in responding to global climate change. The Spirit convicts USA politicians of their complicity in "legal" lawlessness when police and public officials take a knee in solidarity with protestors. Spirit is found in the empathetic and empowering words of politicians, priests, and professors and she also exposes the pretenses of the powerful and elite presenting an alternative to our death-dealing institutions and challenging our divisiveness.

We can never control or claim to know the movements of the Spirit. With Unitarian pastor Theodore Parker, we must be agnostic and humble in confessing that the moral and spiritual arc is beyond our comprehension. In words that apply to Spirit, whose presence inspires our adventures in moral evolution, Parker confesses:

I do not pretend to understand the moral universe, the arc is a long one, my eye reaches but a little ways. I cannot calculate the curve and complete the figure by the experience of sight; I can divine it by conscience. But from what I see I am sure it bends towards justice.

The Spirit inspires a passionate agnosticism and humble intensity that inspires change while respecting diverse and contrasting visions. Recognizing our own limitations as well as the ubiquity of Spirit, we can both protest and pray and innovate and include,

---

7 For theological reflection in a time of pandemic, see Bruce Epperly, *Faith in a Time of Pandemic* (Gonzales, FL: Energion, 2020) and *Hope Beyond Pandemic* (Gonzales, FL: Energion, 2020).

challenging compassionately our own finite perspectives and temptation to absolutize our viewpoints as well as the limitations of those with whom we contend, hoping for reconciliation within prophetic protest.

CHAPTER FOUR

GLOBAL SPIRIT

> God is not far from each one of us. For in him "we live
> and move and have our being," as some of your poets have
> said. (Acts 17:27-28)

Fifty days after Easter flames and wind descended on Jesus' first followers. Although they had been promised the coming of an Advocate and Comforter and heard from Jesus' lips that they would receive power from above — Spirit Power, God Power, Wisdom Power, Healing Power — the coming of the Spirit surprised Jesus' followers as much as it surprised the multicultural community who first heard their messages. Unfettered spirit turned their lives upside down and then ignited the city of Jerusalem.

They had a message that rocked the world. Quoting the prophet Joel, Peter proclaimed that everything the prophets dreamed of, God's Shalom, would come to pass through the movements of God's Spirit.

> God declares I will pour out my Spirit upon all flesh,
> and your sons and your daughters shall prophesy,
> and your young men shall see visions,
> and your old men shall dream dreams.
> Even upon my slaves, both men and women,
> in those days I will pour out my Spirit;
> and they shall prophesy.

As I write these words on Pentecost Sunday, May 31, 2020, the news is filled with the graphic images of the impact of pandemic and protest. Flames of anger and protest engulf American cities. Peaceful protesters animated by the scene of another unarmed African American male unjustly killed by police officers. On this day, celebrating the lively breath of the Spirit embracing all creation and humankind in its wondrous diversity, the cries "I can't breathe" echo in our collective psyche. Denying the unfettered and animating breath of Spirit, choking the divine out of our fellow humans, we fall into violence, traumatizing millions of African Americans, deeply wounded by America's original sin of slavery and four centuries of systemic racism.

God's Restless Spirit births the dream of a new heaven and a new earth. It is not escape, but healing and transformation of persons and politics so that God's heavenly vision, God's vision of wholeness and Shalom, is manifest in earthly life. The Restless Spirit midwives a democracy of revelation and with it a universality of affirmation. God's voice is heard in the voiceless and broken. God's breath whispers in all whose voices are stifled and spirits asphyxiated by vapid worship, deadly orthodoxy, and social injustice. God's wisdom resonates in the imaginations of children and the prayers of protesters, imagining a more perfect union and more heavenly earth.

The global is also personal. God's Spirit comes to us in ways we can understand and in the insights of our culture and religious traditions. On that first Pentecost, God's Spirit transcended parochialism, including the Aramaic language of Jesus' first followers.

> Now there were devout Jews from every nation under heaven living in Jerusalem. And at this sound, the crowd gathered and was bewildered, because each one heard them speaking in the native language of each. Amazed and astonished, they asked, "Are not all these who are speaking Galileans? And how is it that we hear, each of us, in our own native language? (Acts 2:5-8)

Everyone experiences the Spirit in their own language. The Spirit honors diversity and speaks through the intricate and dynamic kaleidoscope of human experience. In the life of the Spirit, there is no "other." Challenging uniformity of experience or interpretation, the centered pluralism of God's nature is revealed in the many manifestations of God's Spirit.

On that first Christian Pentecost, God's Spirit showed the world what it looks like to embody God's realm of Shalom. Positively put, God's Spirit affirms every child as God's beloved. Every culture and ethnic community is a unique recipient of divine blessing, with the gates of salvation open to all. Women and men alike carriers of wisdom. Children can be prophets and teenagers can be environmental sages.

Peter is affirming, with Nicolas of Cusa and Bonaventure, that God is a circle whose center is everywhere and whose circumference is nowhere. There is no outside to God's love, inspiration, and salvation. Everyone is in the circle, everyone embraced, everyone the object of divine blessing, even when we run away from it or side with naysayers and dividers.

Every affirmation has a shadow negation. Organized Christianity is still a long way from embodying God's dream of Shalom. Indeed, there are moments when Christians intentionally turn their backs on the Spirit, promoting dishonesty, incivility, and divisiveness in relationships and in the body politic. Put negatively, Peter's message asserts that a follower of Jesus must mindfully — though often imperfectly — aim at rooting out every vestige of racism, sexism, classism, heterosexism, and elitism to embrace "that which is of God," as the Quakers say, in everyone. The mysticism of the Spirit defies and challenges every structure of exclusion and injustice, every politics that stifles a child's imagination and robs them of a parent's love. The universality of revelation leads to the universality of affirmation from which emerges the universality of moral consideration.

God's universal revelation takes us beyond every binary perspective and welcomes us to a world where everyone is an insider and can repent and embrace God's way, from Donald Trump to Greta Thunberg and George Floyd to Derek Chauvin. God's global Spirit ushers in a world in which everyone can confess and be born anew and every nation ask forgiveness and mend its ways so that justice rolls down like waters.

After dreaming of a ladder of angels, ascending from earth to heaven and back to earth, Jacob exclaimed "God was in this place — and I did not know it." Every place is a portal to Divinity. Everyone is God's child, but we often don't know it. Every person whom we challenge politically and relationally is God's child and we — and they — often do not know it!

In the life of the Spirit, the personal is the political, and the political is the personal. As the first followers of Jesus discovered,

Peter's words condemned the acceptance of any second-class status in the church. There is no Jim Crow or separate but equal in the church. No back row or segregated balcony. All must have freedom in the Spirit or none can truly claim spiritual or personal freedom. The Spirit of God blows through church itself and embraces the whole earth, relativizing our faith, doctrines, and polities in relation to God's diverse and universal revelation. The universalist spiritual reformer, Paul of Tarsus, believed God's Spirit breathes in all of us so that we can affirm that:

> There is no longer Jew or Greek,
> there is no longer slave or free,
> there is no longer male and female;
> for all of you are one in Christ Jesus.
> (Galatians 3:28)

Beyond the binary is unity and harmony, an intricate and dynamic symphony of divine revelation. Today we might expand Paul's words to affirm:

> In Christ,
> there is no longer citizen or undocumented resident,
> there is no longer black or white,
> there is no longer aged or young,
> there is no longer gay or straight,
> there is no longer transgendered or cisgendered,
> there is no longer human or non-human,
> there is no longer police or protestor,
> there is no Christian or Muslim,
> for you are all one in God's global spirit.

Divine revelation even goes beyond both church and humankind. Following Psalms 148 and 150, we live in a world of praise in which all creation praises its Creator, with its own unique voice. Revelation is everywhere and can be found in every creature. "All things are words of God," German mystic Meister Eckhardt proclaims. Beyond the binary, we can lovingly claim our unity in the Spirit and affirm that they will know we follow Jesus by our love.

Spirit in Creation — Beyond Humankind and Church. The wind over the waters moves through all creation, beyond both humanity, Christianity, and any religious tradition. The Spirit that groans in humankind is also groaning in the creation's labor pains. (Romans 8:23) While God's Spirit works uniquely in our quest for wholeness, our experience of the Spirit is continuous with the Spirit's movements in all things. All creation, and the fourteen billion-year evolutionary process, bear the dynamic inspiration of Spirit, described as Sophia and Chokmah in Proverbs 8:

> The Lord created me at the beginning of his work,
>   the first of his acts of long ago.
> Ages ago I was set up,
>   at the first, before the beginning of the earth.
> When there were no depths I was brought forth,
>   when there were no springs abounding with water.
> Before the mountains had been shaped,
>   before the hills, I was brought forth—
> when God had not yet made earth and fields,
>   or the world's first bits of soil.
> When God established the heavens, I was there,
>   when the Creator drew a circle on the face of the deep,
> when God made firm the skies above,
>   when God established the fountains of the deep,
>   when the Holy One assigned to the sea its limit,
>   so that the waters might not transgress
>   the Divine command,
> when God marked out the foundations of the earth,
> then I was beside the Creator, like a master worker
>   [or little child];
> and I was daily God's delight,
>   rejoicing before the Creator always,
>   rejoicing in God's inhabited world
>   and delighting in the human race. (Proverbs 8:21-31)

If, as I believe, Wisdom, described as Logos or the Divine Creative Word in John's Gospel, is another word for the Holy Spirit, then Creative Wisdom, Sophia, brings forth the world in delight.

22

The universe reflects not only the moral and spiritual arc of divine justice-seeking, but the playfulness of God. The Spirit inspires the universe toward greater beauty just as the Spirit challenges humankind toward greater moral and spiritual stature. Spirit subtly moves through our cells as well as through the yearnings of our souls for more abundant and fulfilling life. The Spirit evolves the non-human world toward greater intensity of experience in the slow path of evolution and likewise seeks, though with greater challenge and resistance, a similar ethical and spiritual evolution in humankind and its institutions.

The Voice from the Whirlwind to Job proclaims a diverse, evolving, dynamic, intricate, dangerous, and amazingly wonderful universe that inclines us toward praise, prayer, and playfulness. (Job, chapters 38–41) How can we not delight in the Spirit's midwifing the creation of behemoth and leviathan, Pleiades and Orion, and wild ass and ostrich? How can we not feel the thrill of the Navajo wise one, gazing into the horizon, and proclaiming "with beauty all around me I walk?" How can we not savor our embrace of the Beautiful God, described by process theologian Patricia Adams Farmer?[8]

Playful creativity undergirds the serious business of spiritual transformation. Though we may turn from the Spirit's Way, drowning out Wisdom's call, and pursuing the ways of death, Spirit's promise to those who hear her voice is life in all its abundance and the opportunity to claim their role as Spirit's companions in healing the world. (Psalm 8:1, 32-36)

---

8 Patricia Adams Farmer, *Embracing a Beautiful God* (St. Louis: Chalice Press, 2003) and *Beauty and Process Theology* (Gonzales, FL: Energion Books, 2020).

CHAPTER FIVE

GUIDING SPIRIT

> Likewise, the Spirit helps us in our weakness; for we do
> not know how to pray as we ought, but that very Spirit inter-
> cedes with sighs too deep for words. (Romans 8:26)

God's Spirit is Infinite and Intimate. There is virtually no limit to the manifestations of the Spirit in our lives and the world. The political movements of the Spirit are personal, challenging us to create structures of wholeness that break down the walls of race, economics, religion, age, gender, and sexuality. The personal movements of the Spirit are also the political insofar as the Spirit whispers or rages in each life calling us to balance our well-being with the wellbeing of our communities and the planet. While the Spirit moves within the non-human world evoking the gifts of our companion animals as well as our companions on land and sea, most especially among chimpanzees, gorillas, whales, and dolphins, inspiring them toward realizing their highest selves, this chapter will focus primarily on the Spirit's aims at human wholeness.

With the cross on the horizon, Jesus promises that the Spirit will guide and sustain his followers both individually and as a community.

> I will ask the Father, and he will give you another
> Advocate [Helper] to be with you forever. This is
> the Spirit of truth whom the world cannot receive,
> because it neither sees him nor knows him. You know
> him because he abides with you, and he will be in
> you…you will know that I am in my Father, and you
> in me, and I in you. (John 14:16-17, 20)

While not exclusive to followers of Jesus, the emerging community of Jesus, or churches today, those who follow Jesus will experience what others neglect, the inner wisdom and energy of God. As Peter's Pentecost speech asserts, God's Spirit is available to

24

all. Wholeness is God's gift to all, but the call of the Spirit requires our response to be fully actualized in our lives.

Surely, the Spirit is working anonymously in every life. When we open to the Spirit, aligning ourselves with the Spirit's vision, God's wisdom becomes ours, opening us to the fruits and gifts of God's Spirit, uniquely available to each person. Alfred North Whitehead captures the God's call and response in a way that illuminates Jesus' words to his first followers:

> God's purpose is always embodied in particular ideals relevant to the actual state of the world...Every act leaves the world with a deeper or fainter impress God. He then passes to his next relation to the world with enlarged, or diminished, presentation of ideal values.[9]

Though God's Spirit is always personal, it is nurtured by Spirit-centered communities, whose purpose is not only to reveal the Spirit to the world but nurture the Spirit in individuals. Paul describes life in the Spirit as faithful and free, oriented to life rather than death, and expansive rather than self-interested. Life in the Spirit is oriented toward God's values in the world, transcending the fleshly orientation toward self-interest, greed, and materialism, to embody God's vision of wholeness "on earth as it is in heaven."

We must be clear that embodied life is a gift of God. Spirit is earthy as well as transcendent. Bodies are good, sensuality is good. Spirit is as present in our physical activity and political protest as in fasting and contemplating. The connection of Spirit (pneuma) with breath points to the intimacy of the Spirit, which is more than intellectual, it is also emotional, volitional, and sensory, addressing the totality of our being in our current situation.

A movement toward the Spirit, emerging through personal spiritual practices and community nurture, elicits encounters with the Holy. Paul describes the mysticism of the Spirit, emerging from Christian community, as an intimate companionship with God in which our identity becomes shaped by the Spirit's movements in our lives.

---

9 Alfred North Whitehead, *Religion in the Making* (New York: Meridian Books, 1972), 152.

When we cry "Abba, Father," it is that very Spirit bearing witness with our spirit that we are children of God, and if children, then heirs, heirs with God and joint heirs with Christ. (Romans 8:15-16)

After awakening from a dream of a ladder of angels, the patriarch Jacob exclaims God was in this place and I did not know it. The same can be said for the Spirit. The Spirit is always moving in our lives, but most of the time its presence is unnoticed or beneath the surface of consciousness. Through prayer, meditation, commitment to faithful community, and attentiveness to the holiness of our daily lives, the Spirit becomes a decisive factor in our self-understanding and behavior. Spirit guides us unconsciously and consciously, luring us toward our vocation in God's Holy Adventure.

Likewise the Spirit helps us in our weakness; for we do not know how to pray as we ought, but that very Spirit intercedes with sighs too deep for words. And God, who searches the heart, knows what is the mind of the Spirit, because the Spirit intercedes for the saints according to the will of God. (Romans 8:26-27)

Spirit is always moving in our lives and when we turn toward the Spirit, whose "sighs are too deep for words," always moving beneath the surface of consciousness, the Spirit comes alive, awakening us to the fruits and gifts of her presence. What was guiding us unconsciously now becomes our Spiritual GPS orienting us toward God's vision for our lives and our role in healing the world.

Fruits of the Spirit. God's Spirit is profoundly practical in shaping our lives. Those who attend to the Spirit, awakening to its graceful energy and wisdom, can manifest more than they can imagine in their personal lives and social involvements. Jesus asserts that we are all connected to God and that through a process of pruning our lives in partnership with God we will bear much fruit.

I am the vine, you are the branches. Those who abide in me and I in them bear much fruit, because apart from me you can do nothing. (John 15:5)

The Apostle Paul sees the fruit of God's Spirit as a way of life — a process of orienting our behaviors and attitudes so that they bring joy to us and those around us. The fruit of the Spirit is intended to go public in shaping our relationships and involvements.

> The fruit of the Spirit is love, joy, peace, patience, kindness, generosity, faithfulness, gentleness, and self-control. (Galatians 5:22-23)

While the fruits are interpersonal, creating healing and life-supporting relationships, they also are political. Our relationships extend far beyond our immediate neighbor and family member. Inner joy and peace issue in loving relationships, reflecting abundant patience and self-control. The Spirit's fruits mature in gentleness in our immediate circle of friends and family.

Living out this quest to embody spiritual fruit has been especially important to me in the relative solitude of writing this text during the Spring and Summer of 2020, in the middle of a time of pandemic and protest. But, beyond small circle of family with whom I directly interact in gentle and supportive ways on a daily basis, my commitment to exhibiting the fruit of the Spirit must also be manifest in kindness, gentleness, generosity, and love in the larger circle of social relationships and political involvement. These virtues of daily life must eventuate the quest to "do justice, love kindness, and walk humbly with your God" (Micah 6:8) whether as a citizen seeking political change or posting on social media.[10]

Gifts of the Spirit. Pastor and author Frederick Buechner asserts that "the place that God calls you to is the place where your deep gladness and the world's deep hunger meet." Living in companionship with God's Spirit awakens us to the vocation of each unique moment as well as vocational gifts occurring in our specific life season as well as over a lifetime. Our gifts are intended for our fulfillment and joy and for the well-being of the relationships and communities of which we are a part. 1 Corinthians 12 is the most extended and, I believe, inspirational description of the gifts of God's Spirit. The Apostle Paul proclaims:

---

10 For a spirituality of social media, see Bruce Epperly, *God Online: A Mystic's Guide to the Internet* (Vestal, NY: Anamchara Books, 2020).

Now there are varieties of gifts, but the same Spirit; and there are varieties of services, but the same Lord; and there are varieties of activities, but it is the same God who activates all of them in everyone. To each is given the manifestation of the Spirit for the common good. (1 Corinthians 12:4-5)

While Paul enumerates the gifts of explicit Christian community — teaching, preaching, healing, wisdom, ecstasy, discernment, and spiritual understanding — this roster of gifts is not intended to be exhaustive but an invitation to develop our unique leadership gifts. Nor are these gifts restricted to Christians. Within the dynamic, interdependent, and constantly creative Body of Christ, not unlike our own bodies, there are multitudes of gifts. Every aspect of the Body of Christ, or our human bodies, has a vocation that contributes to the health of the organism. (1 Corinthians 12:8-11)

The Energy of the Spirit flows through our cells as well as our souls to bring wholeness and agency. (1 Corinthians 12:12-31) Everyone is gifted. Everyone, regardless of life experience, intellectual acuity, physical ability, gender, race, and sexuality, reflects the Spirit's inspiration. In fact, our differences — like the differing organs and systems of the body -are essential to the functioning of the whole.

Within community, our gifts are intended to bless others individually and collectively and in turn bless us. No gift is individual or isolated, all are nurtured by and shape the larger whole whether it is the human organism, body, mind, and spirit, or a congregation, community, nation, and planet. Nothing is more personal and intimate than the Spirit's movements. Conversely, nothing is more global and relational than the Spirit's embodied presence. The Spirit is the inspiration of the Beloved Community in which "if one member suffers, all suffer together with it; if one member is honored, all rejoice together with it." (1 Corinthians 12:31) As we will see in the next chapter, in this intersection of personal growth and community health, the prophetic Spirit emerges, binding us together in the affirmation "God in all things, all things in God."[11]

11 For more on spiritual gifts see Robert D. Cornwall, *Unfettered Spirit: Spiritual Gifts of the New Great Awakening* (Gonzales, FL: Energion Publications, 2020).

CHAPTER SIX

PROPHETIC SPIRIT

> He has told you, O mortal, what is good;
>> and what does the Lord require of you
> but to do justice, and to love kindness,
>> and to walk humbly with your God? (Micah 6:8)

God's Spirit turns everything upside and reorients our values. While profoundly personal, speaking within our individual gifts and relationships, the Spirit creates a beloved community among those who embrace its wisdom. In creating a community of unfettered compassion and revelation, Jesus seamlessly and transparently embodied God's wholeness in such a way that the Creative Parent, Incarnate Word and Wisdom, and Restless and Prophetic Spirit of God were present in every act. Accordingly, it was appropriate that Jesus' first public message channeled the Spirit present in the prophet Isaiah:

> The Spirit of the Lord is upon me,
>> because he has anointed me
>>> to bring good news to the poor.
> He has sent me to proclaim release to the captives
>> and recovery of sight to the blind,
>>> to let the oppressed go free,
> to proclaim the year of the Lord's favor. (Luke 4:18-19)

The prophetic Spirit awakens us to the distance between God's vision of Shalom and personal and corporate waywardness and injustice. The Spirit reflects the Divine Pathos, described by Abraham Joshua Heschel as God's pain at the reality of poverty, injustice, and violence. Both Infinite and Intimate, the Spirit initiates and midwives alternative possibilities to the injustice often systemically enshrined in our political and economic systems as well as our own quests for personal and relational wholeness. While there may be a "sweet, sweet Spirit in this place," the peace of the Spirit joins loving and inspired worship with profound restlessness and critique of leaders and institutions that perpetrate injustice.

The restlessness of the Spirit is captured by singer-songwriter and spiritual leader Jim Manley:

Spirit, Spirit of gentleness,
blow through the wilderness, calling and free.
Spirit, Spirit of restlessness,
Stir me from placidness, wind, wind, on the sea.

You swept through the desert.
You stung with the stand,
and you goaded your people with a law and a land,
and when they were blinded with their idols and lies,
then you spoke through their prophets to open their eyes.

Unfettered and on the move, God's Spirit challenges every relational and institutional barrier to experiencing the fullness of God's presence. Those who experience the Spirit's breathing seek to make it possible for all God's children to breathe deeply God's freedom and fulfill lovingly God's giftedness in their lives. The Spirit sets us free from the laws of sin and death, individually but more importantly institutionally, breaking down structures of injustice and oppression. (Romans 8:2)

Prophetic Spirit as Pragmatic. Spirit inspires us to action. The Wisdom and Word of God, Sophia, and Logos, is incarnate in the messy world of politics, economics, and personal decision-making. Inspired by the Pentecost Spirit, the first followers of Jesus became champions of economic equality. If divine inspiration is universal, the democracy of the Spirit must lead to economic and relational democracy. If salvation is open to all persons, so must the possibility of social and economic equality.

> Awe came upon everyone because many wonders and signs were being done by the apostles. All who believed were together and had all things in common; they would sell their possessions and goods and distribute the proceeds to all, as any had need. Day by day, as they spent much time together in the temple, they broke bread at home and ate their food with glad and generous hearts, praising God and having the goodwill of

all the people. And day by day the Lord added to their number those who were being saved. (Acts 2:43-47)

The prophetic justice of the Spirit, transcending the false separation of contemplation and action is so important to Jesus' Spirit-filled followers that the communal economics of the Jerusalem community is mentioned twice:

> Now the whole group of those who believed were of one heart and soul, and no one claimed private ownership of any possessions, but everything they owned was held in common. With great power the apostles gave their testimony to the resurrection of the Lord Jesus, and great grace was upon them all. There was not a needy person among them, for as many as owned lands or houses sold them and brought the proceeds of what was sold. They laid it at the apostles' feet, and it was distributed to each as any had need. (Acts 4:32-35)

Unity of spirit leads to economic equality in the Christian movement and lures us toward economic justice in the marketplace and halls of government. In a Spirit-filled world, everyone is blessed not only by God's Spirit but by our uplifting of each other. No one is left out of the community's success. No one is forgotten in terms of congregational or communal largesse. No one is second class. Although the Spirit inspires relational and behavioral guideposts, the Spirit's intent is to create an environment where everyone can experience and express the gifts of the Spirit for their own fulfillment and the well-being of the community. Spirit joins, while the demonic separates. Spirit unites, while self-interest divides. In opening to the flow of the Spirit individually and institutionally, we become partners giving life and energy to the body of Christ in our midst. While practicalities of life need to be worked out flexibly for each family, congregation, community, and nation, not to mention the Spirit's dream of planetary unity, every personal and institutional action must have as its goal the vision of God's Shalom "on earth as it is in heaven." Accordingly, economic and judicial inequality, environmental destruction, and systemic injustice are sins against God's Spirit which call for repentance and transformation among persons and nations. Ultimately this turning toward the ways of the Spirit will lead to the goal of prophetic healing as

31

the goal of social critique and protest. Compassionate challenge always leaves the door open for permanent reconciliation.

CHAPTER SEVEN

HEALING SPIRIT

I came that they might have life, and have it abundantly.
(John 10:10)

The Holy Spirit is always restless and prophetic. God's Spirit challenges our personal and communal barriers to experiencing the fullness of God's grace. The mysticism of the Spirit, embodied in the still, small voice, quiet sighs, and ecstatic flames and tongues, drives us from our personal and political siloes out into the streets with a message of unity and transformation. Emerging from the heart, the Spirit activates our hands and feet to march toward the Zion of God's vision of Shalom, "on earth as it is in heaven." Awakening our gifts, the Spirit inspires us to see our vocations — the living out of deep gladness and giftedness — as joining self-actualization with community wellbeing.

Energized by the Spirit, Jesus proclaimed his personal mission statement, which bears repeating in our time of protest and pandemic, in his first public message:

The Spirit of the Lord is upon me,
    because he has anointed me
    to bring good news to the poor.
He has sent me to proclaim release to the captives
    and recovery of sight to the blind,
        to let the oppressed go free,
    to proclaim the year of the Lord's favor. (Luke 4:18-19)

Every aspect of the Spirit's movements aims at healing persons and communities, and creating structures of the Spirit to promote Jesus' other mission statement in daily life and the affairs of nations — "I came that they may have life, and have it abundantly." (John 10:10) Abundant life is a promise for each and for all, not unlike still-to-be-fulfilled American dream of "life, liberty, and the pursuit of happiness."

Healing comes to earth when the poor hear good news of economic justice, captives prosecuted and victimized by unjust social structures are liberated, those with their backs against the wall are free at last, and those limited by sight impairment and other illnesses cured and able to become agents of their destinies. Jubilee attends the movements of the Spirit as she seeks to bring forth a world in which everyone has an equal starting point to live out their gifts to bring health to their communities.

Spirit heals whether that healing touches our cells, souls, or cities. Jesus was a healer whose healing touch restored broken bodies and whose love activated faithful agency among those he encountered. In Jesus' healing ministry, healing of body, mind, spirit, and social standing were interconnected. When a woman with a flow of blood touches Jesus, the energy of love flows through her curing her physical ailment. Just as important was the healing of her religious and social situation. Now she was no longer unclean and unable to attend religious services, interact with friends, or have intimate relations with her husband. When Jesus proclaimed the healing of lepers, their bodies were restored and so was their place in society. No longer having to cry out their uncleanliness as they approached strangers or lived at the margins of society, they could return to homes, jobs, and synagogues fully functioning within the social and religious structures.

Jesus' healing ministry embraced the outsiders, whether the wealthy tax collector Zacchaeus, a man emotionally terrorized by demonic powers, or a woman caught in adultery. Embracing the unclean and marginalized, Jesus acted as Spirit's emissary bringing the lost to their rightful homes and communities, bringing them from the center to the margins. The Good Shepherd searches ceaselessly for the hundredth sheep not only to save the lost one from certain catastrophe but to bring wholeness to the ninety-nine who will be incomplete without the hundredth companion.

Spirit heals. Prophets cry out against the rich and powerful so that their hearts will be transformed and greed transplanted by generosity. Jesus protests profit-making in the Temple so that everyone, rich and poor, healthy or sick, can come to God's realm equally. Paul challenges the religious legalists in Galatia so that every follower of Jesus can sit in the front row, enjoying equal status in God's realm on earth as it is in heaven.

The Spirit's healing is never binary in nature. Individual physical and emotional recovery requires changed hearts and attitudes. Protesting injustice promoted by the powerful and privileged uplifts the poor but enables the unjust to hear God's voice in their lives. Spirit-filled salvation is Pentecostal in nature. There are no outsiders in the realm of God's healing Spirit. All are welcome and the well-being of one and all are connected. Healed communities promote healthy spirits and spirits touched by God's Spirit work for the justice and equality necessary for personal wellbeing.

Even in the spiritual paradise of the first Christian community where people sold their goods and shared everything in common, healing is still needed. As the community grew, perhaps to the size of a small village, the Greek-speaking members of the community protested that the Hellenistic widows were being neglected in the distribution of food, threatening their physical and spiritual wellbeing. (Acts 6;1-6) Rather than being defensive the Hebraic leadership prayed for communal transformation, appointed spirit-filled leaders to ensure equity, and healed a potential schism. The Spirit is concerned with the healing of economics and ethnicity as well as our personal lives.

The Spirit's universality was put to the test once more when Peter had a vision of unclean food, protested God's invitation to share in the buffet, and then was told to call nothing unclean. Shortly after his vision, emissaries from Cornelius, a Gentile military leader, arrived on Peter's doorstep. A seeker after truth and salvation, their Gentile employer had also had a vision, telling him to seek out Peter. When Peter and Cornelius finally meet, the ecstasy of the Spirit descends on Jew and Gentile alike. The walls of race and ethnicity were broken down, as they were earlier with Philip and the Ethiopian eunuch, widening the circle of salvation to embrace all humankind. If God accepts people from every nation, then this must also be our mandate as Spirit-inspired Christians. Walking in the Spirit, we become God's healing companions, addressing diseases of body, mind, spirit, economics, politics, and ecology.

CHAPTER EIGHT

THE FURTHER ADVENTURES OF THE SPIRIT

"Go out and stand on the mountain before God, for God is about to pass by." Now there was a great wind, so strong that it was splitting mountains and breaking rocks in pieces before God, but God was not in the wind; and after the wind an earthquake, but God was not in the earthquake; and after the earthquake a fire, but God was not in the fire; and after the fire a sound of sheer silence. When Elijah heard it, he wrapped his face in his mantle and went out and stood at the entrance of the cave. Then there came a voice to him that said, "What are you doing here, Elijah?" (I Kings 19:11-13, AP)

We are living in a perfect storm of upheaval and uncertainty. Some of it is immediate, as current as today's headlines — pandemic, structural racism and injustice, protest, and the politicization of science. Other aspects of the storm engulfing us are more subtle but just as challenging to what once was the status quo — global climate change, loss of a sense of common good and national unity, and the twilight of Christian exceptionalism.

Iconic stores and brands are going out of business, victims of pandemic and technology. Our recreational and culinary habits have been turned upside down. We wonder, "Is dinner and a movie a thing of the past?" Eager to go out, we ask "when will we feel comfortable returning to our favorite restaurant or vacation spot?" When will we feel comfortable boarding a six-hour plane flight for business or pleasure? For good reason, policing as we know it is "under fire" and the call for radical transformation of police forces and the justice system fills the air.

The church in North America is in upheaval. Prior to the pandemic, the role of Christianity in shaping culture was already in decline, with the growth of religious diversity; the emergence of the "nones" and "dones" for whom institutional religion has become irrelevant; and the ubiquity of non-institutional seekers, describing themselves as spiritual but not religious. This decline has been exacerbated by the identification of Christians as anti-science, anti-

36

gay, anti-fact, anti-democracy, and anti-diversity by many young persons and their senior seekers. You might even say such attitudes are anti-Spirit!

Christian exceptionalists cry persecution over any incursion on their "right" to worship any time and place they wish despite health risks and any infringement on their ability to deny civil rights to the LGBTQ+ community or non-Christian religious tradition. Cake decorations and marriage licenses become the stuff of culture wars. Even wearing face masks has become a dividing line between progressive and conservative Christians. Needless to say, this martyrdom complex sullies the reputation of the way of Jesus in the public media and among seekers.

Within mainstream and progressive Christianity, the impact of the cultural maelstrom is just as significant. Our voices are often neglected by the media, which chooses controversy over day-to-day fidelity to the gospel. We are uncertain how to creatively integrate the current cultural upheaval into our theological and homiletical reflections. Theological reflection and spiritual formation need to maintain a critical distance even from the movements we support, preventing us from baptizing our political preferences as God's perspective. Moreover, we have silenced theological, spiritual, and ethical diversity by our own litmus tests, questioning the good faith of our allies over minor differences in theological or political perspective or deviations from our perspectives. All of this is emerging in the context of our concerns about whether our congregations, denominational bodies, and institutions will survive the pandemic.

Spirit-centered progressive Christians have been faithful to our affirmation of science and concern for safety. We have appropriately shuttered our doors for public worship and returned to public worship practicing safe distancing, wearing masks, and encouraging vaccinations. Yet, we wonder when and if we will come back, knowing the future of the ministerial profession and congregational mission are at stake. We have initiated, as Whitehead counsels, novelty to match the novelties of our time, but we also yearn for a return to normalcy and our particular congregational traditions, while knowing that "normal" is unlikely to return to our worship services and missional practices. In this maelstrom of change, God asks progressive Christians and process theologians, "What are you doing here?"

Like the author of Psalm 46, we are seeking to be faithful and courageous in our commitment to the way of Jesus "though the earth should change, though the mountains shake in the heart of the sea; though its waters roar and foam, though the mountains tremble with its tumult…though the nations are in an uproar, though the kingdoms totter." (Psalm 46:2-3, 6) In these moments of spiritual and cultural upheaval, the Psalmist counsels us to "be still, and know that I am God." (Psalm 46:10) The Spirit is found in both stillness and storm, and in the center of the cyclone, we pause to get our spiritual bearings for the challenges that lie before us.

To chart the further adventures of the Spirit is, of course, a daunting, if not impossible, task. The Spirit blows where she wishes and cannot be contained by our theological perspectives. Still, with humility, we can claim that the treasures of the Spirit flow through earthen vessels, the imperfect visions and practices of our churches, theological reflections, and spiritual practices.

Sightings on the Pilgrimage. As I began the seminar that led to the writing of this text, it was clear that most Spirit-seekers were both monastics and pilgrims during the days of protest and pandemics. We were monastics, sheltering in place. In my case, no longer holding public worship services and able to visit homes, hospitals, and nursing homes, most of my days were spent in my home, reading, writing, providing educational and relational resources for my young grandchildren, and teaching classes and conducting worship Zoom. I ventured out at sunrise for a walk on a Cape Cod Beach, drove to the home of my son and his family, and walked our 85-pound Golden Doodle in the neighborhood. As the song says, "I Don't Get Out Much Anymore," as we had our groceries and adult beverages delivered contactless to our home. It was normal for baby boomers, senior adults, and families with children to live a type of monastic existence.

We may have been monks during the time of pandemic but we were also pilgrims of the Spirit, trying to keep up with the latest information about the pandemic, appalled at police violence and presidential ineptitude and polarization, and pondering with our congregants and other pastors what church would look like in the year ahead. We were wandering but were not necessarily lost, to quote J.R.R. Tolkien, as we sought the Spirit's guidance on our unique personal, congregational, and political holy adventures. We experienced Spirit-sightings and imagined where Wisdom would lead us. We glimpsed contours of the Spirit, guided by past encounters described by the mystics of scripture, prophetic protestors, and moments of insight in our own lives and in the spiritual autobiography. We cannot fathom the depths of the Spirit, for she is more than we can ask or imagine. But I believe we can glimpse the movements of Spirit rustling through our city streets, village greens, over the waters, and in our own deep breathing. I believe we can train our eyes for Spirit sightings in:

- *Voices of prophetic protest.* The Spirit often moves anonymously in sighs too deep for words. Not bound by church or doctrine, it can show up among followers of Jesus and non-Christians protesting injustice. Surely God's spirit is in the protests following George Floyd's death, the Poor Peoples Campaign and Moral March under the leadership of Rev. William Barber, the March for Our Lives for gun safety, the Friday walkouts led by Greta Thunberg. Absent from Bible-toting photo ops, the Spirit speaks for the poor, vulnerable, marginalized, violated, oppressed. The Spirit speaks for the voiceless in inner cities, refugee camps, and Appalachian hollers. The Spirit speaks in the songs of the Humpbacked Whale and the pain of endangered species.
- *Moments of self-transcendence and creativity.* The Spirit is felt in our own sighs too deep for words, in moments of creativity and mysticism which invite us to a larger vision. Mysticism leads to mission. When people encounter God, they get a job. They receive a vocation to be God's companion in healing the earth.
- *The Interplay of Unity and Diversity.* The Spirit inspires diverse groups to join in common cause. God loves diversity, whether in the creation of the universe or the Pentecost phenomena of hearing the one message in many ways. We

have church whenever we are one in the Spirit. In April 2020, America was protesting, as people of all colors and age groups, often with whites outnumbering blacks took to the streets seeking justice and challenging racism. Spirit is sighted in all the colors of the rainbow declaring their unique gifts proudly, giving thanks for the giftedness of life, and affirming all the other, including newly-discovered, colors of the rainbow as companions on a holy adventure. The Spirit calls us to see the unity in diversity and affirm the diversity in unity. The Spirit delights in pluralism, promoting the varied gifts of persons and communities. Listening to the Spirit means training our senses to see the unique gifts of those around us as well as our need to work together to heal the planet. *Ubuntu, "I am because of you. We are because of one another."*

- *Dedicated earth caring and planetary healing.* An unexpected effect of the pandemic was the appearance of bluer skies and less carbon dioxide in the environment due to decreased fossil fuel consumption. Sadly, many dis-Spirited USA leaders want to offset these gains by relaxing environmental regulations. Spirit loves flesh. Spirit gives life to all things. Spirit-Wisdom delights in creation, speaking through pangolins, penguins, porcupines, and porpoises. Radical amazement is the only response to Spirit-sightings in the non-human world. Spirit inspires a world of praise and calls humankind to praise Wisdom for her gifts in the non-human world.

- *Touches that Heal.* God's Spirit touches creation with love. Just as Jesus touched lepers and allowed himself to be touched by unclean women, Spirit inspires every healing touch from a grandparent cradling a crying child, lovers embracing each other, physicians and nurses comforting patients, researchers creating vaccines, and friends and fellow worshippers offering reiki healing touch and laying on of hands. Even in a time of safe distancing, we can touch our hearts as signs of affirmation, we can open our arms as a sign of God's healing embrace. We can fold our hands in prayer and say "peace be with you" or "Namaste" to express the energy that enlightens and embraces. We can touch the earth lightly, walking with beauty all around us and bringing beauty to this wonderful but turbulent earth.

Acts of the Apostles, also known as the book of the Holy Spirit, concludes with words describing the Apostle Paul's freedom, despite imprisonment. No prison wall could prevent him from "proclaiming the kingdom of God and teaching about the Lord Jesus Christ with all boldness and without hindrance." (Acts 28:30) This is our calling as we become companions in the further adventures of God's Wise and Creative, Unfettered and Liberating Spirit, moving "without hindrance" through us and all creation to share good news, heal the broken, awaken the apathetic, protest, and rejoice in the beauty of the earth.

Topical Line Drives

Straight to the point in 44 pages
https://topicallinedrives.com